The Book of Exodus: God's Commandments in Colors

The Book of Exodus: God's Commandments in Colors

Developed by

Gary R. Brown

Paperback: ISBN 979-8-9902592-0-1

Edited by (Gary R. Brown/PleaseLetThemKnow, L.L.C.)
Cover Art by (Gary R. Brown/PleaseLetThemKnow, L.L.C.)
Layout by (Gary R. Brown/PleaseLetThemKnow, L.L.C.)

Printed in the USA

Dedication

I dedicate this book to three critical people in my life. Firstly, my beloved mother, Marjorie Clark Brown, instilled in me a love for literature and faith. Secondly, my precious daughter India Brown inspires me to create and share my passions. And lastly, my dear friend Veronica McCottrell, whose unwavering support and encouragement have been a constant source of strength and motivation. To all of you, I offer my love and gratitude.

Acknowledgments

I sincerely thank my fantastic mom, Marjorie Clark Brown, my wonderful daughter, India Brown, and my dearest friend, Veronica McCottrell, for their unwavering support and encouragement while creating my project on the Book of Exodus. Their inspiration, guidance, and contributions were invaluable, and I am so grateful for their love, patience, and understanding. This project and many others would not have been possible without their assistance and contributions. I feel incredibly blessed to have them and am thankful for their unwavering support.

Table of Contents

Preface

The Book of Exodus has always fascinated me with its vivid imagery and powerful message. As a lover of literature and faith, I have been drawn to this story of a people seeking freedom and redemption from a life of oppression and slavery. The classic film The Ten Commandments also inspired me with its striking visual images that brought this epic tale to life on the big screen.

In my new book, The Book of Exodus: God's Commandments in Colors, I hope to capture the essence of this timeless story. Illustrations and commentary bring to life Moses' journey and the Ten Commandments as the Israelites journey to the promised land.

I hope the book will inspire readers to rediscover the power and relevance of this ancient tale and reflect on the timeless truths it contains about faith, freedom, and the human spirit. Whether you are a student of religion, a lover of literature, or someone seeking inspiration and guidance in your life, the story of Exodus has something to offer everyone.

Join me on this journey through the Book of Exodus and discover the power and beauty of God's Commandments in Colors.

Introduction

I am happy to introduce my latest project, "The Book of Exodus: God's Commandments in Colors." This book captures the timeless wisdom and powerful message of the story of Moses and the Israelites' journey from slavery in Egypt to the Promised Land. Through vivid illustrations and colorful interpretations, this book brings this story to life in an engaging and informative way. It highlights the importance of forgiveness, unity, and trust in God, as demonstrated by the Israelites' journey through the desert.

The Ten Commandments, one of the most well-known Bible references, are also featured in the book. I hope it will inspire readers to explore the Bible further and seek a deeper understanding of its teachings. As it is written in Exodus 20:3-17, "You shall have no other gods before me..." and in Exodus 14:14, "The Lord will fight for you, and you have only to be silent." These verses, among many others, illustrate the importance of faith, obedience, and trust in God's plan for our lives.

Exodus 3:14-15

God said to Moses, "I am who I am. This is what you are to say to the Israelites: 'I am has sent me to you.'"
God also said to Moses, "Say to the Israelites, 'The Lord, the God of your fathers—the God of Abraham, the God of Isaac and the God of Jacob—has sent me to you.'
"This is my name forever,
the name you shall call me
from generation to generation.

Chapter 1: The Israelites in Egypt

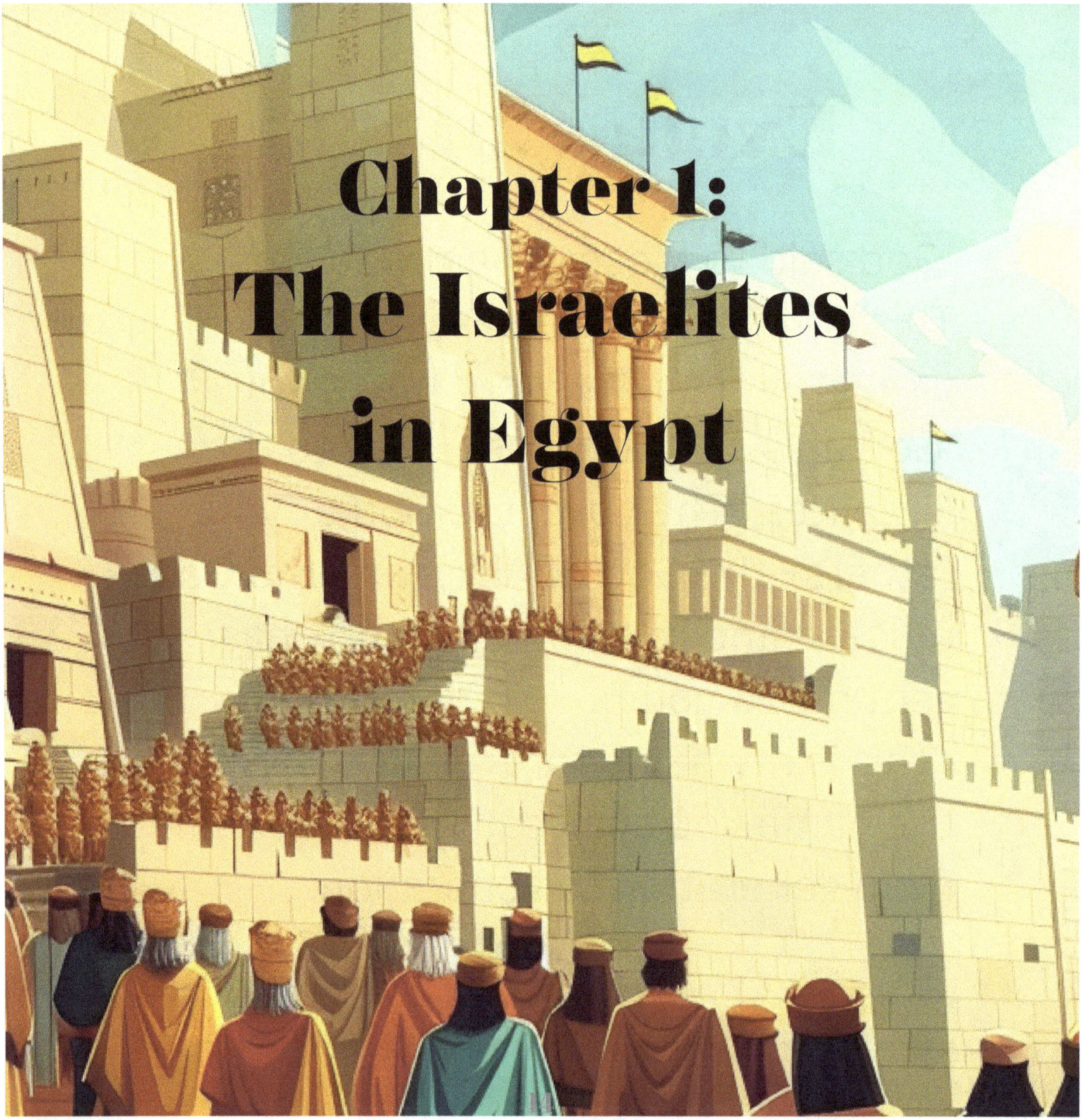

In ancient times, the Israelites lived in Egypt and enjoyed a happy life. They had migrated to Egypt to escape a famine in their country, and over time, they grew into a large and prosperous community. This prosperity worried the Egyptians, who feared the Israelites becoming too powerful. As a result, they forced the Israelites to work as slaves, subjecting them to harsh treatment and forcing them to perform complex tasks daily without any compensation. This went on for a long time. (Exodus 1:14).

The Pharaoh, the ruler of Egypt, was particularly concerned about the Israelites' growth and decided to make their lives even harder. He wanted to weaken them and keep them under his control. The Israelites struggled to work hard under cruel conditions, building significant buildings and statues that glorified the Pharaoh. Despite being slaves, the Israelites continued to grow in number, which made the Egyptians even more fearful.

The situation became unbearable for the Israelites, and they prayed to God for help. They knew that God had promised their ancestors they would have their land, and they hoped that God would help them escape Egypt and go to that land. Their prayers were answered, and God sent Moses to lead the Israelites out of Egypt. in the Book of Exodus, chapter 2, verse 23: "During that long period, the king of Egypt died.

The Israelites groaned in their slavery and cried out, and their cry for help because of their slavery went up to God." The Israelites' cries and prayers were heard by God, and He sent Moses to deliver them from the hands of the Egyptians.

Chapter 2: Moses & the Burning Bush

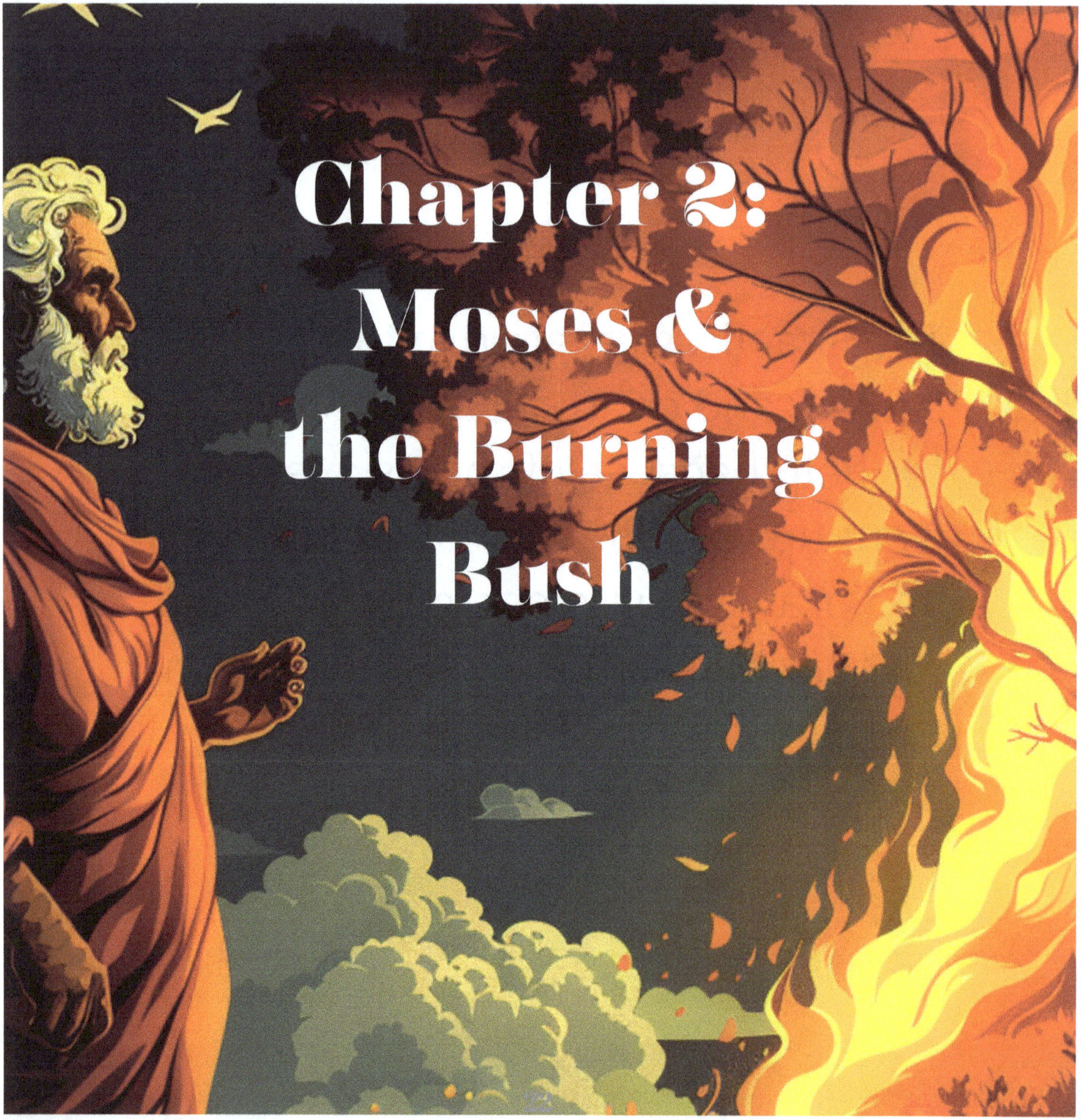

The story of Moses and the Burning Bush is pivotal in the Book of Exodus. As Moses was tending to his father-in-law's flock, he saw a bush on fire but not being consumed. As he approached the bush, he heard the voice of God calling out to him. In Exodus 3:5-6, God instructed Moses to remove his shoes out of respect as he stood on holy ground. God then revealed his plan to Moses, telling him that he had chosen him to lead the Israelites out of Egypt and into the Promised Land.

Despite feeling unworthy and unsure of his abilities, Moses accepted the task, and God reassured him that he would be with him every step of the way. The story of Moses and the Burning Bush is significant for many reasons. It shows how God can reveal himself unexpectedly and use ordinary people to do extraordinary things.

It also highlights the importance of trust and faith in God's plan, even when we may feel inadequate or unsure. The story of Moses and the Burning Bush is a decisive moment in the Book of Exodus that sets the stage for the rest of the story. It shows how God can work through individuals to accomplish his purposes and reminds us of the importance of listening to his voice and following his guidance.

Chapter 3:
The Plagues

The Ten Plagues of Egypt are a significant part of the Book of Exodus from the Bible. As it is written in Exodus 7:14 through 12:36, God sent ten plagues to Egypt to convince the Pharaoh to release the Israelites from slavery and let them go to the Promised Land. Each plague was a devastating punishment that affected the Egyptians' daily life, but the Israelites were spared.

The Nile turned to blood, frogs covered the land, gnats, and flies infested the air, livestock died, boils broke out on people and animals, hail and fire rained from the sky, locusts devoured the crops, darkness covered the land, and finally, the firstborn of every Egyptian household died. After the tenth plague, the Pharaoh finally agreed to let the Israelites go, and they could leave Egypt and begin their journey to the Promised Land. The story of the Ten Plagues of Egypt is an emphatic reminder of God's justice and mercy.

It teaches us that God will intervene to help us overcome oppression and suffering. It also reminds us of the importance of heeding God's will and respecting human freedom. As it is written in Exodus 9:16, "But I have raised you up for this very purpose, that I might show you my power and that my name might be proclaimed in all the earth." The Ten Plagues of Egypt are a testament to the human spirit and the resilience of those who trust God's guidance.

1. Water turned into blood: God turned the Nile River and all the water in Egypt into blood, making it undrinkable and killing all the fish.

2. Frogs: Frogs covered the land, filling houses and beds everywhere.

3. Lice: All the dust in Egypt turned into lice, infesting people and animals.

4. Flies: Swarms of flies covered the land, making it impossible to work or live.

5. Livestock disease: All the livestock in Egypt died, leaving the Egyptians without any valuable resources.

6. Boils: Painful boils appeared on the skin of the Egyptians, causing immense suffering.

7. A Thunderstorm of hail and fire rained down on Egypt, destroying crops and buildings.

8. Locusts: Swarms of locusts devastated the crops and vegetation, leaving nothing for the Egyptians to eat.

DARKNESS

Exodus 10:13
 No one could see anyone
else or move about for three
days. Yet all the Israelites
had light in the places where
they lived.

9. Darkness: A thick darkness covered Egypt for three days, so thick that the Egyptians could not see anything.

10. Death of the firstborn: The most devastating plague of all, this plague resulted in the death of the firstborn son in every Egyptian household, including the Pharaoh's son.

After the tenth plague, the Pharaoh finally agreed to let the Israelites go, and they could leave Egypt and begin their journey to the Promised Land.

Chapter 4: Crossing the Red Sea

The Crossing of the Red Sea is one of the Bible's most iconic and memorable events. After the Israelites were freed from their slavery in Egypt, they were faced with a new challenge. Pharaoh had a change of heart and decided to send his army after the Israelites to bring them back to Egypt. The Israelites were trapped between the Egyptian military and the Red Sea, with seemingly no way out. However, God miraculously parted the waters of the Red Sea, creating a dry path for the Israelites to cross safely to the other side. The Crossing of the Red Sea story is significant for several reasons.

Firstly, it portrays God's supremacy and the ability to perform miracles to help his people. Exodus 14:21-22 says, "Then Moses stretched out his hand over the sea, and all that night the Lord drove the sea back with a strong east wind and turned it into dry land. The waters were divided, and the Israelites went through the sea on dry ground, with a wall of water on their right and left." This verse is a testament to God's power and ability to work miracles.

Secondly, the story emphasizes the importance of faith and trust in God. The Israelites had to rely on their faith and trust that God would provide a way out of their predicament. This is true for us as well. When we face insurmountable challenges, we must remember to trust in God, who will guide us through our struggles.

Finally, the Crossing of the Red Sea foreshadows baptism in the Christian faith. Christians believe that baptism delivers them from sin and death and into eternal life, just as the Israelites were delivered from slavery and chaos through the Red Sea. The story is a reminder that God can provide a way of escape even in the face of seemingly impossible obstacles.

Overall, the Crossing of the Red Sea story is a powerful and inspiring testament to God's power, faithfulness, and provision.

Chapter 5:
The Ten
Commandments

The Ten Commandments, also known as the Decalogue, are a set of laws God gave to the Israelites through Moses on Mount Sinai in the Book of Exodus (Exodus 20:1-17). These commandments are considered the foundation of Jewish and Christian morality and ethics and have influenced the laws and values of many societies throughout history. Each commandment serves as a rule of behavior and conduct, providing believers a moral and ethical framework to follow. For instance, the first commandment states, "You shall have no other gods before me" (Exodus 20:3), emphasizing the importance of monotheism and the belief in one true God.

The fifth commandment states, "Honor your father and your mother" (Exodus 20:12), recognizing the importance of family relationships and requiring the respect and honor of parents.

The Ten Commandments also emphasize personal responsibility and respect for others. For example, the sixth commandment prohibits the taking of another person's life, emphasizing the sanctity of human life (Exodus 20:13). The eighth commandment prohibits theft. It emphasizes respecting other people's property and possessions (Exodus 20:15).

Moreover, the Ten Commandments serve as a reminder of the importance of a deep and meaningful relationship with God. The fourth commandment requires the observance of the Sabbath, a day of rest and worship, emphasizing the importance of spiritual renewal and rest (Exodus 20:8-11).

The Ten Commandments remain relevant today as a guiding force for individuals and societies seeking to live a just and ethical life. They provide a clear and concise set of principles that promote morality, ethics, and personal responsibility, emphasizing the importance of a deep and meaningful relationship with God.

Here is a detailed explanation of the Ten Commandments:

1. "You shall have no other gods before me." This commandment emphasizes the importance of monotheism and the belief in one true God. It forbids the worship of idols, false gods, and anything that may take the place of God in a person's life.

2. "You shall not make for yourself an image in the form of anything in heaven above or on the earth beneath or in the waters below." This commandment further emphasizes the prohibition of idolatry and the worship of physical images and statues.

3. "You shall not misuse the name of the Lord your God." This commandment prohibits using God's name in vain or for frivolous purposes. It emphasizes the importance of reverent and respectful behavior towards God.

4. "Remember the Sabbath day by keeping it holy." This commandment requires the observance of the Sabbath, a day of rest and worship. It emphasizes the importance of spiritual renewal and rest.

5. "Honor your father and your mother." This commandment recognizes the importance of family relationships and requires the respect and honor of parents.

6. "You shall not murder." This commandment prohibits the taking of another person's life and emphasizes the sanctity of human life.

7. "You shall not commit adultery." This commandment prohibits sexual infidelity and emphasizes the importance of faithfulness and commitment in relationships.

8. "You shall not steal." This commandment prohibits theft and emphasizes respecting other people's property and possessions.

9. "You shall not give false testimony against your neighbor." This commandment prohibits lying and bearing false witness against others. It emphasizes the importance of truthfulness and integrity.

Exodus

Oppressed

he names of the sons of Is-
went to Egypt with Jacob,
family: [2]Reuben, Simeon,
h; [3]Issachar, Zebulun and
n and Naphtali; Gad and
escendants of Jacob num-
in all; Joseph was already in

nd all his brothers and all
ed, [7]but the Israelites
and ultiplied greatly and
dingly numerous, so that the
with them
w king, who
came to power in Egypt.
aid to his people, ''the Israel-
me much too numerous for
e must deal shrewdly with
will become even more nu-
war breaks out, will join our
against us and leave the

slave masters over them to
with forced labor, and they

more numerous. [21]And because the mid-
wives feared God, he gave them families of
their own.

[22]Then Pharaoh gave this order to all his
people: ''Every boy that is born[b] you must
throw into the Nile, but let every girl live.''

The Birth of Moses

2 Now a man of the house of Levi mar-
ried a Levite woman, [2]and she became
pregnant and gave birth to a son. When she
saw that he was a fine child, she hid him for
three months. [3]But when she could hide
him no longer, she got a basket for
him and coated it with tar. Then
she placed the child in it and put it among
the reeds along the bank of the Nile. [4]His
sister stood at a distance to see what would
happen to him.

[5]Then Pharaoh's daughter went down to
the Nile to bathe, and her attendants were
walking along the river bank. She saw the
basket among the reeds and sent her slave
girl to get it. [6]She opened it and saw the
baby. He was crying, and she felt sorry for

10. "You shall not covet your neighbor's house. You shall not covet your neighbor's wife, or his male or female servant, his ox or donkey, or anything that belongs to your neighbor." This commandment prohibits envy and the desire for things that belong to others. It emphasizes the importance of contentment and gratitude.

The Book of Exodus Summary

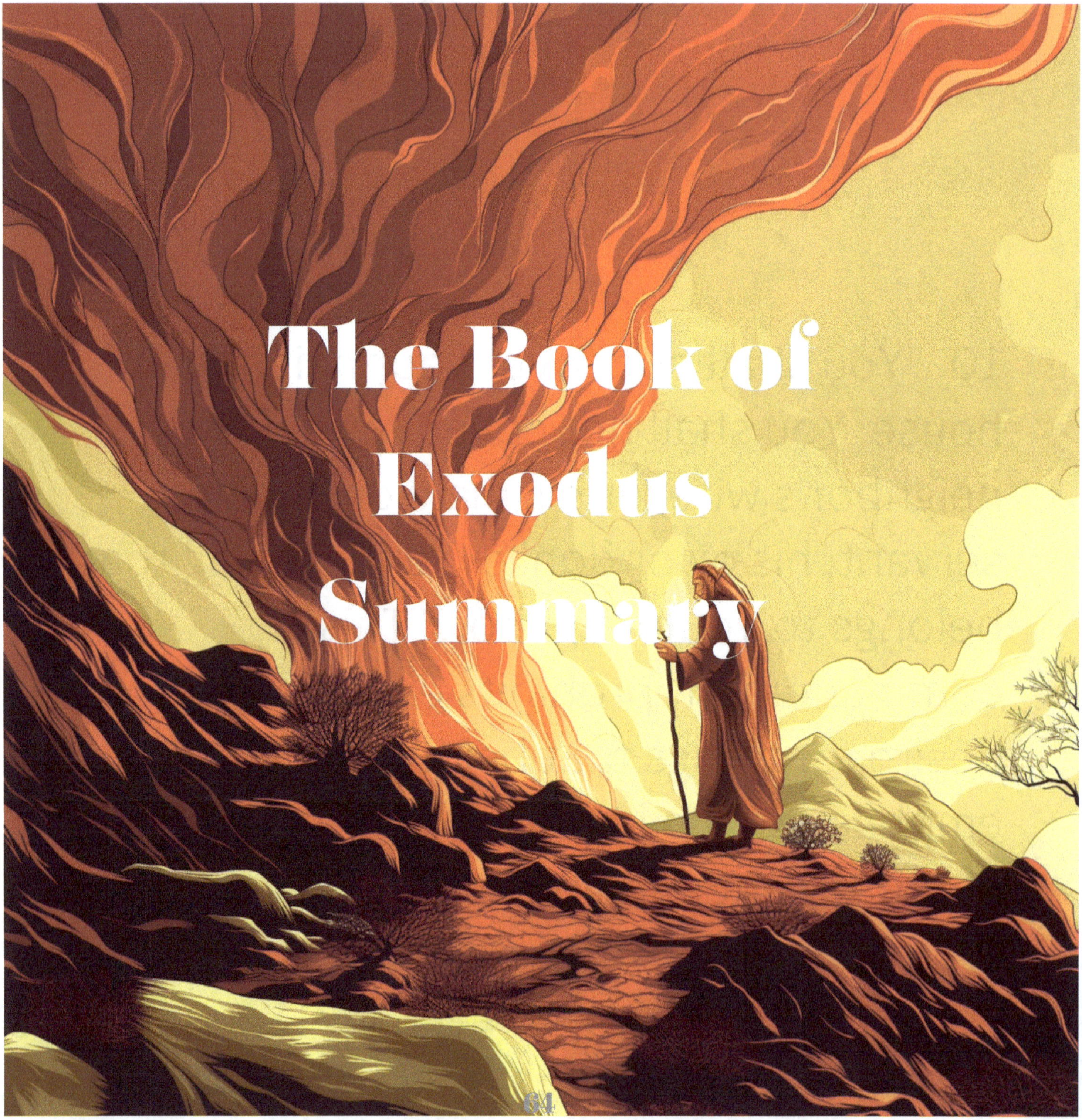

The Book of Exodus is an influential narrative of hope, faith, and deliverance. It recounts the story of the Israelites' journey from slavery in Egypt to freedom in the Promised Land, providing a rich and vivid depiction of their daily lives as enslaved people. In Exodus 3:10-12, God chooses Moses, a humble shepherd, to lead the Israelites out of Egypt, and we see how God's guidance and intervention played a crucial role in their liberation.

The ten plagues God sent on Egypt, described in Exodus 7-11, symbolize God's power and justice. They serve as a reminder that God is faithful to His people and will always stand by them in times of trouble.

The story also introduces the Ten Commandments, the foundation for many world legal systems. In Exodus 20:1-17, God delivers these commandments to Moses on Mount Sinai, revealing a code of conduct emphasizing respect for God, oneself, and others.

Overall, the Book of Exodus is a story that transports us to a different time and place, allowing us to experience the Israelites' journey as if we were with actually there!

An Afterword

As we come to the end of this journey through the Book of Exodus, it is essential to reflect on the messages and perspectives that have been shared. Through the plights of the Israelites, the Ten Commandments, and the continued journey, we have seen how listening, faithfulness, and patience in the face of God can lead to redemption and deliverance.

The colorful depictions of the Commandments in this book are a reminder of the importance of following God's laws and living a righteous life. The plagues the Egyptians endured show us that those who oppress others will face consequences for their actions.

Perhaps most importantly, the continued journey of the Israelites reminds us that our faith is not a one-time event but a journey that requires perseverance and dedication. We must continue to listen to God's voice and trust in His plan for our lives, even when things seem uncertain or complex.

I hope this book has given you a deeper understanding and appreciation of the Book of Exodus. May it inspire you to live a life of faithfulness, righteousness, and compassion, just as the Israelites did as they journeyed through the wilderness.

Why the Bible

I have always had a deep affinity for the Holy Bible and its messages of hope, faith, and redemption. Over time, I have found various ways to share this love with others, such as creating word search puzzles, crossword puzzles, and other games based on biblical themes. Recently, I decided to take this passion to the next level by writing books about my Christian faith. My first book, The Book of Exodus: God's Commandments in Colors, conveys the essence of this timeless story through colorful illustrations and insightful commentary.

My ultimate goal is to inspire readers to rediscover the power and relevance of the Bible's teachings. Through my writings, word search books, crossword puzzles, and other activities, I encourage readers to reflect on the timeless truths in its pages. With a particular focus on faith, freedom, and the human spirit, we can undertake a journey of exploration and discovery together. The Bible's rich history and message of hope and redemption can guide us toward a more fulfilling life. So let us delve deeper into its pages with an open mind and heart and discover the treasures.

About the Developer

PleaseLetThemKnow, LLC is a small business that offers a wide range of books suitable for all age groups. Our product line includes medium, low, and original works, available on Amazon's Kindle Book Publishing service. Our founder, Gary R. Brown, a retired U.S. Navy member, started this business in March 2023 to offer books, games, journals, and puzzle books for both children and seniors. We follow a cost-saving structure that benefits everyone and ensures our prices remain affordable.

At PleaseLetThemKnow, we believe in expanding our reach to bring our books to larger populations and areas. We always seek partners who share our vision and can help us achieve our goals. You can visit our website at www.pleaseletthemknow.com for more information and to explore our collection. Thank you for supporting our small business!

www.ingramcontent.com/pod-product-compliance
Lightning Source LLC
LaVergne TN
LVHW061336060426
835511LV00014B/1950